CARS!

EVERYTHING YOU NEED TO KNOW: LOCKED DOWN!

SCHOLASTIC

Answers:

Page 6: Car Crazy
1. a / 2. c / 3. true / 4. all of them / 5. c

Page 18: Collision!
1. Fiat (g) / 2. Toyota (d) / 3. Honda (j)
4. Hyundai (a) / 5. Chevrolet (f) / 6. Jaguar (h)
7. Cadillac (i) / 8. Porsche (h) / 9. Volkswagen (e)
10. Mercedes (c)

Page 30: Cool Car Clash
Car B wins!

Page 54: Hidden Cars

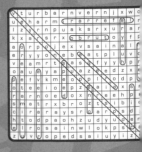

CONTENTS

CAR CRAZY

People have been crazy about cars since they first roared onto our roads. But how much do you really know about these mean machines? Are you a true petrol-head or an absolute beginner? Buckle up as we find out in this quiz. You'll find the answers on page 4.

1. When did the first cars hit the road?

a) The 1890s ✓

b) The 1930s

c) The 1790s

2. What speed did the Hennessey Venom GT achieve in 2014?

a) 190 mph

b) 216 mph

c) 270 mph ✓

3. True or false? In Britain, cars had been on the road for more than 40 years before anyone had to sit a driving test.

4. Which of these methods can be used to power a car?

a) Cooking oil

b) Petrol

c) Liquid gas

5. How many cars are estimated to be on the world's roads today?

a) 167,000

b) 1,000,000

c) Over 1,000,000,000

CHAPTER 1
CREATING CARS

People have travelled on wheels for thousands of years and for most of that time things were pulled by horses. It is only in the last 130 years or so that horses have been replaced by engines. Lots of different people had a hand in inventing cars – so let's take a journey back through history and see how these early cars started.

THE FIRST CARS

Who invented cars? It's not as simple as you'd think. Up until the 1700s, horses had done the hard work, but the invention of steam and electric engines created new ways to power things. But neither were very practical or reliable. It was only with the development of petrol power that people began to think that the car might catch on after all...

EARLY CAR ENGINE

EARLY PEUGEOT, 1896

BENZ MOTOR CAR, 1886

1885
Three wheels or four?

The German inventors Karl Benz and Gottlieb Daimler each make petrol-powered carriages. Benz's has three wheels, and Daimler's has four. Both machines are often called the 'first cars'.

1890s
The first car companies

In France, Panhard et Levassor form a company in 1889, followed by Peugeot in 1891. In the United States, the Duryea brothers start the first American company to make cars. Back in Europe in 1898, Daimler opens a workshop in Germany.

FAST FACT

Early cars were made by hand, one at a time. This meant they were expensive to make and for people to buy. By 1913, Henry Ford changed this by using an assembly line to make his cars. Dozens of workers each added one or two parts to the car as it moved along a conveyor belt. Cars became cheaper and faster to make.

Whose Car?

Like Ford, many early car-making companies were named after their owners. You might recognize some of these names on cars today...

Louis **CHEVROLET**

Walter P. **CHRYSLER**

John and Horace **DODGE**

Enzo **FERRARI**

Henry **FORD**

Soichiro **HONDA**

Ferdinand **PORSCHE**

Louis **RENAULT**

André-Gustave **CITROËN**

Karl Friedrich **BENZ**

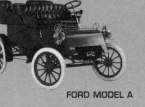

FORD MODEL A

FORD MODEL T

1903
Here comes Ford

American Henry Ford puts out the Model A car. It is a well-made car, but it still sells only a couple of thousand. Half of all the cars in the world are being made in France, but by the following year, car production in the US overtakes Europe.

1908
Booming!

Ford's Model T bursts onto the market. His new way of building cars on an assembly line means cars are cheaper to make and buy. The car becomes a huge hit.

NOW WE'RE MOVING

The Ford Model T kicked off a boom in car making. The Model T, or 'Tin Lizzie' as people called it, was able to cope with rough, unfinished roads. It was simple, but strong and reliable. Better still, the car was becoming more affordable.

LUXURY

Model As and Model Ts were for everyday drivers. But really rich people wanted to travel in style. Many even employed a chauffer to do the driving for them in their luxury cars made by companies such as Rolls-Royce, Bugatti and Talbot-Lago.

1911
No more cranks

CAR STARTED WITH A CRANK

Until 1910, cars had to be started with a special handle called a crank. The driver used it to spin a starter at the front of the car. It had to be done carefully – get it wrong and the force was enough to break the driver's arm. Thankfully, Charles Kettering got around this by inventing an electric starter, which was much easier, not to mention safer!

1931
Fewer bounces

Remember those rough dirt roads? This year, Mercedes-Benz invented a way for each front wheel to move up and down on its own. This made the ride smoother for drivers and passengers, as the car didn't shake about quite so much.

FAST FACT

In the late 1800s and early 1900s, most cars were open-topped; that is, they had no roofs. By the 1930s, however, most cars were closed in. But that wasn't the end of open-top cars altogether. They became a style statement in the form of flashy convertible sports cars!

MERCEDES 300 SL ROADSTER

EARLY CAR INDICATOR

WORLD WAR II CORSAIR FIGHTER AIRCRAFT

CLASSIC 1950s CHEVROLET BEL-AIR

USING HAND SIGNALS

1935
Left turn!

How do you know if the car in front of you is about to turn? You see a blinking light. But it was not until 1935 that cars had that important safety feature. Before then, people just used hand signals!

1950s
War inspiration

In the USA this was the age of huge cars with cool fins and shining chrome. Meanwhile in Europe, people were still recovering from World War II. Money was tight, so car-makers concentrated on creating smaller models that were cheaper to buy and run.

CARS TODAY

From the 1960s onwards, car designers started to replace the sharp fins with smooth lines. In the United States, 'pony cars' – smaller, sleek two-door cars – became popular. In Britain, the bestselling Mini Cooper was launched. It was a real hit, thanks to its compact size and trendy design.

1980s HONDA CIVIC

1970s
MINI COOPER

1970
Clean it up

Car engines produce lots of pollution. In the 1970s, tough new standards were brought in to reduce pollution. Manufacturers had to make cleaner engines that release fewer harmful chemicals. Since then, people have been trying to make the car cleaner and greener.

1980s
A new number 1

For the first time in history, the United States was not the top car-producing country. It was overtaken by Japan, with brands such as Toyota and Honda. In Britain, the success of the Mini led many companies to launch their own small cars such as the Ford Fiesta, Austin Metro and the Peugeot 205. At the luxury end of the market, Porsche launched the legendary 911.

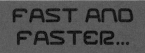

NOW THAT'S SMART!

The Smart car was introduced in 1997. It only fits two people and is less than half as long as a standard two-door, which means it can squeeze into the smallest of parking spaces – even parking at right angles to the kerb!

FAST AND FASTER...

Since Ford's sales of a few thousand Model Ts in 1908, car sales have accelerated at an amazing rate...

Year	Worldwide Car Sales
1920	2.4 million
1950	10.8 million
1970	29.7 million
2000	41.2 million
2005	67 million
2014	71 million

2000s
SUVs and compact city cars

Sport utility vehicles (SUVs for short) took off, bringing the tough look of 4 x 4 off-roaders to the streets. But not everyone wanted big cars. Designers were still trying to make greener vehicles and the compact city car became popular because they used less fuel and were also easier to park.

EARLY TOYOTA PRIUS

1990s
New ways to move

Electric and hybrid cars entered the market. People wanted new ways to drive that didn't pollute the environment as much as petrol cars. Toyota leads the way with the Prius.

2014
Another new number 1

China made about 23 million cars in 2014, more than any other country in the world.

MAKING A CAR

An average car has more than 30,000 separate parts. All of them have to be put together just right or the car won't work. Modern cars are made in factories by hundreds of workers. Many factories also use robots to help put the cars together. But a car's journey doesn't start at the factory, it begins with an idea called a 'brief'. Let's take a look at the key stages in creating a new car.

1) The Brief

Any car, whether it's a change to an existing car or a completely new shape, starts with a brief for the design team. This might be 'Come up with an exciting new car for a family', for example.

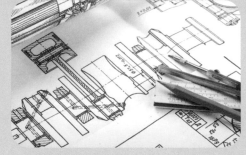

2) Planning

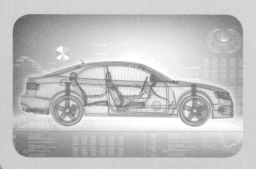

The designers will start with simple sketches on paper or on a computer screen, which may take months of planning and changes. Sometimes, the end model that goes on sale is very different from the first plans on screen.

3) Play With Clay

Once everyone is happy with the design, model-makers create it in clay at a much smaller size. They look at it from every angle to see if the design works. Some car-makers use 3D printers, too.

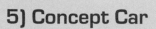

4) Prototype

This is a full-scale model. Made from metal or plastic, the car is now full-size, but it's still a model.

5) Concept Car

Some car companies make a one-off car called a 'concept car'. This is displayed at car shows to see what people think of it. The company may make more changes to the car before it goes into production.

6) On The Line

Once the model is perfect inside and out, a plan is made for all the parts the car will need. Once the parts are made, it's time to go to the assembly line. Workers and robots put the parts of the car together one at a time as it moves on a conveyor belt.

7) Ready To Roll

And here it comes! Fresh out of the factory, a beautiful new car, ready to hit the roads.

ENVIRONMENTAL CARS

Not Just Petrol!

Petrol engines put out a lot of exhaust fumes. These are gases created by the engine as it runs. With more than a billion cars on the planet, that's a lot of pollution. Scientists know that all those exhaust fumes are really bad for living things and our planet. So car-makers are looking at some cleaner ways to make cars go.

Electric Cars

People wanted new ways to drive that didn't pollute the environment as much as petrol cars, so makers launched electric cars. These are powered by a battery, which is recharged at a special outlet. Other makers launched hybrid cars, such as the Toyota Prius, which uses both petrol and electricity.

Hybrid Cars

Hybrid just means made from more than one thing. So the Prius has both a battery and a petrol engine and can switch between EV (electric vehicle) mode and normal mode. The battery charges while the engine is running. Hybrids use less fuel and create much less air pollution than normal cars.

FAST FACT

Some creative people have figured out a way to use cooking oil to run cars. They collect the oil from restaurants, then it is converted into bio-fuel. Some restaurants use the recycled oil to power some of their trucks – that's real fast food!

Natural Gas Cars

Instead of liquid petrol, which is made from oil, another fossil fuel called natural gas makes these cars run. Natural gas burns more cleanly than petrol but, like petrol, it still comes from fossil fuels, which will eventually run out.

Solar-Powered Cars

Car designers have been trying to work out how energy from the Sun – solar power – can be used to run cars. It's clean and there's plenty of it, but it may be some time before the first cars are ready to hit the road.

COLLISION!

Below you'll find the scrambled names of several well-known car makes. Can you work out which is which and then match them to the right badge? The answers are on page 4.

a

b

c

d

e

f

g

h

i

j

1. IFAT

2. OOTTYA

3. NDOAH

4. YADIUHN

5. VELTREOHC

6. GAJURA

7. LICCALAD

8. CHEPROS

9. GOSAVVWEKNL

10. SCEERDME

CHAPTER 2
CARS INSIDE AND OUT

From smooth lines, to polished paintwork and not forgetting awesome extras like alloys and spoilers... It's easy to love a car for its look alone. But what's going on underneath that gleaming metal? It's time to put on your overalls as we pop the bonnet and explore the mass of machinery inside.

ENGINES

With the turn of a key or the press of a button, a car's engine comes roaring to life. It may seem amazing, but it's just science at work. Making a car move starts with the fuel and the engine. Let's take a closer look.

Every time a car starts, it kicks off a series of mini explosions. That's right... turn the key, and KAPOW! In most petrol- or diesel-powered cars, there are four to 12 cylinders (although the Bugatti Veyron has 16!). The more cylinders, the more power. Cylinders go through what's called a 'four-stroke cycle'.

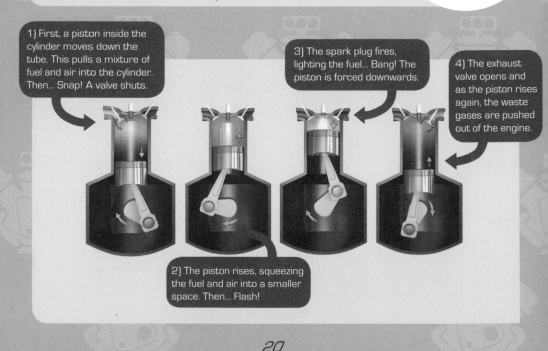

1) First, a piston inside the cylinder moves down the tube. This pulls a mixture of fuel and air into the cylinder. Then... Snap! A valve shuts.

2) The piston rises, squeezing the fuel and air into a smaller space. Then... Flash!

3) The spark plug fires, lighting the fuel... Bang! The piston is forced downwards.

4) The exhaust valve opens and as the piston rises again, the waste gases are pushed out of the engine.

Each cylinder in the engine fires in sequence very quickly. This keeps a rod called the crankshaft spinning at high speed, which turns the wheels.

FAST FACT

With all these mini explosions, it's important cars don't get too hot! So they have special liquid called coolant flowing around the engine. It soaks up the heat and takes it back to the car radiator, where metal fins absorb the heat and push it into the air outside.

Smooth Running

All the moving metal in an engine needs something to keep it running smoothly. This is the job of engine oil. As an engine warms up, the oil does too. This makes it thin so it flows around, coating all the metal parts so they move freely.

FAST FACT

Cars may have replaced horses, but they're still a tiny bit involved in the story. When people talk about the power of a car, they use a measurement called 'horsepower'. This is roughly the same amount of energy as the work of one horse. So a car that has a 210-horsepower engine can do the work of 210 horses.

In the days before cars, most carriages had wooden wheels covered in leather or metal. This made for a really bumpy ride! This began to change in the 1840s, when Charles Goodyear invented vulcanized rubber. It was used for lots of things, including solid wheels. But it was in the 1880s that things would start to get a bit more comfortable, thanks to plain old air...

Early Days

When John Dunlop first figured out a way to put air into tyres it was for his son's tricycle rather than a car. But people quickly saw that air-filled 'pneumatic' tyres would really help to smooth the journey for passengers. The first tyres had an inner tube of air, with an outside rubber casing to protect it. The outside of the tyre had diagonal layers of fabric embedded in the rubber to strengthen the tyre and make it hard-wearing. By the 1950s this was replaced by 'radials' – tyres that have steel cords instead.

FAST FACT

Early pneumatic tyres were a pain if they had a flat. The driver had to heave the tyre off the wheel to repair the inner tube. Luckily someone came up with the idea of carrying a 'spare', which meant it could just be swapped and the flat could be fixed later.

Pump It Up!

Have you ever seen a driver checking the air pressure in their tyres? It's important to keep them at the right levels. If the tyres are too soft they wear out faster. If they are too hard, there will be less of the tyre touching the road, which could make the car harder to control, as well as giving passengers a bumpy ride.

Tread Patterns

Early tyres were smooth and narrow, so they had less rubber touching the road. When it rained, cars would skid all over the place. So tyres got wider and people began to put patterned 'treads' on the tyres. These are a bit like the soles of welly boots. The rain is pushed into the grooves so the tyre can still grip the road.

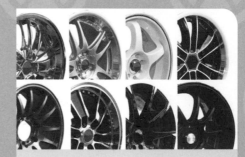

Rolling Bling!

The wheel itself has become part of a car's decoration. Cars can be customized with shiny alloy wheels, bright hubcaps, or even spinning rims. When the car stops, the rims keep spinning, making a cool pattern. See if you can spot any!

INTERIORS

Early cars looked similar to a horse-drawn carriage. The driver and passengers sat high up on bench seats, but at least they were made of padded leather! Today's cars have seats that can be really high-tech, with buttons to alter the height and position. Some can even warm you up on a cold day!

The Talking Car

Almost every new car nowadays has a very active computer inside. It helps control the car's systems . . . and it can even talk to you! The computer can help with directions or let you know when your tyre pressure is low. Some cars can now park themselves. You find a space, line it up and say "park the car". Easy-peasy!

Some cars now look like spaceships! They have dozens of light-up dials, buttons, levers and screens. It takes a smart driver to figure them all out.

Safety First!

Since the first cars, people have come up with all sorts of things to keep drivers and passengers safe. One of the biggest lifesavers has been the seat belt. They were first fitted as standard in the front of cars in the 1960s and since then it is thought they have saved the lives of around a million people. Since seat belts, airbags have also been added to cars to protect people in accidents. If a car crashes, whoosh! They instantly inflate to cushion people.

FAST FACT

Americans love cup holders in their cars. Some minivans have 13 or 14 places to store a drink. You can even get heated cup holders installed!

Awesome Accessories

Here are some of the amazing additions that some people put in their cars to make them feel luxurious:

- Heated seats
- DVD screens and individual headphone jacks
- Mini-refrigerators
- A panoramic roof so you can enjoy the sunshine – or the stars!
- Diamond-studded car keys
- Crocodile-leather trim
- Teak wood floors.

Car fans don't just see a 'car' when a four-wheeled vehicle rolls by. They use all kinds of names for the body shapes. Here's your guide on 'how to talk car'.

Super Mini

These can have two or four doors, but are generally the smallest cars on the road. They usually have very little room in the boot (or trunk in the US). Even-smaller cars are called city cars. *Super mini example:* Toyota Corolla. *City car example:* Smart car.

Saloon

Most cars on the road are saloons. They have four doors and room for five people, including three in the back. They are larger and more comfortable cars with large boots. *Examples:* Mazda 6 or Honda Accord.

Coupé

The original coupés were all low two-seaters. A coupé today can have four seats or even four doors, but they still look fast! *Example:* Porsche Cayman.

SUV

SUV stands for sport utility vehicle. These popular cars (also called 4 x 4s) combine the space of a van or truck with the comfort of a car. They often can fit six or seven people, making them great for families. *Example:* Honda CR-V.

FAST FACT

Some American cars have their own category: muscle cars. They were very popular in the 1960s and 1970s, with big, powerful engines, but sports-car styling. *Example:* Ford Mustang.

Talking Cars Across the Pond

People in the UK and US both speak English, but they have different words for some things in the world of cars.

UK	US
Petrol	Gasoline (Gas for short)
Bonnet	Hood
Car park	Parking lot
Saloon	Sedan
Estate	Station wagon
Lorry	Truck
Boot	Trunk
Windscreen	Windshield
Motorway	Freeway
Petrol station	Gas station

TRUCK CRAZY

Cars are not the only things rolling on the roads. You'll also see vans and pickup trucks, as well as huge 18-wheel lorries thundering along carrying cargo from ports all over the country.

Pickup trucks

They started as work trucks on farms, ranches and building sites. But by the 1960s, pickup trucks were one of the most popular vehicles on the road. Nowadays in the US, many families use a four-door pickup as their main car.

Haulers

Lorries deliver millions of tons of cargo each year. Many are so large they need to run on 18 wheels. The huge container on the trailer can come straight off a ship and onto the lorry . . . and off it goes to market!

Tankers

When carrying liquid – everything from oil to milk to syrup – special tanker trucks are used. They are shaped like cylinders, which is the best shape to hold liquid cargo.

Monster Trucks

Don't look for these on motorways! Specially built monster trucks are used in races and 'freestyle' competitions. Drivers try to see how many cars they can crush with these enormous wheels!

FAST FACT

Did you know that the first monster truck was made in the UK? In the 1950s, the British Forestry Commission needed a truck that could cope with really deep puddles, so designers at Land Rover adapted a model with tractor wheels!

COOL CAR CLASH

Three of the coolest cars ever are at the starting line . . . but they'll each take a different twisting path to the finish. Can you trace their routes and find out who reaches the finish line first?

START

A

B

C

1st

2nd

3rd

CHAPTER 3

THE COOL CAR COLLECTION

Everyone has their own idea of what makes a cool car. It might be a classic 1950s car or perhaps the latest concept supercar. Truth is there are so many amazing cars on the roads today that we would need around 400 pages to include them all. Picking just ten is really tricky, but here is our list of super-cool supercars that most of us can only dream of driving. Once you've read all about them, rank them here:

My Own Cool Car Ranking

1._____

2._____

3._____

4._____

5._____

6._____

7._____

8._____

9._____

10._____

PORSCHE 911

1

Classic lines, a low bonnet, sleek back and a roaring super-fast engine mean the Porsche 911 has long been a favourite since it first hit the roads in 1963. The GT3 RS with its extra-light aluminium body accelerates from 0–60 mph in a jaw-dropping 3.5 seconds, with a top speed of 196 mph. Powered by a 3.8-litre, six-cylinder engine, the GT3 is the ultimate 911!

DID YOU KNOW?

This famous car was 'born' with another name. The first of this model were called Porsche 901s. But another company said that their cars all used zeros in the middle of their names and told Porsche to change! So 901 became... 911!

WOW!

Porsche also makes amazing sports cars. Some of the 911s and other models take part in racing, too. Porsches have won hundreds of races, and it is at the top of the leader board in the 24 Hours of Le Mans race, racking up an incredible 16 wins!

FAST FACTS

Home Country: Germany

Top Speed: 196 mph (315 kph)

Acceleration: 0–60 in less than 3.5 seconds

Horsepower: 475

Price: £100,000+

LAMBORGHINI AVENTADOR

2

Few words mean 'awesome sports car' as much as Lamborghini. For decades, this Italian company has been thrilling drivers and car fans with fast, sleek machines. They don't make very many, which makes seeing them a special treat. The Aventador is the firm favourite of Lambo fans. It has a huge V12 engine – that's 12 cylinders (see page 21). Start saving your pennies for this one. It costs more than £260,000!

FAST FACTS

Home Country: Italy

Top Speed: 217 mph (350 kph)

Acceleration: 0-60 in 2.9 seconds

Horsepower: 691

Price: £260,000+

WOW!

Last year, Italian state police received a Lamborghini Huracan to use as a special squad car for jobs where time – and speed – are key. One of the most important jobs the Huracan is used for is to deliver organs to hospitals for urgent transplant operations.

DID YOU KNOW?

Some of the coolest cars in the world started on a farm! The Italian designer Ferruccio Lamborghini started out making tractors. After he had made enough money building those, he turned to sports cars!

KOENIGSEGG AGERA R

3

Sweden and hot cars are not normally mentioned in the same sentence. Sweden is best known for safe and reliable models like Volvos. But Christian von Koenigsegg decided to change all that. Starting in the mid-1990s, he began designing and building 'hypercars'. Rare, expensive and high-tech, his cars looked fast just standing still. With a carbon-fibre body and an enormous 5-litre turbo-charged V8 engine, the Agera (which means 'action' in Swedish) is jaw-droppingly fast!

DID YOU KNOW?

The Agera R is super-rare with a production run of just 18 cars. Now that's an exclusive club to belong to!

FAST FACTS

Home Country: Sweden

Top Speed: 273 mph (439 kph)

Acceleration: 0–60 in 2.8 seconds

Horsepower: 1,141

Price: £2,000,000

WOW!

Don't blink or you might miss this speed demon! In 2011, an Agera R set a world record by going from zero to 186 mph (300 kph) in only 14.5 seconds!

MCLAREN 650S SPIDER

Best-known for their Formula One cars, McLaren has used their design and engineering skill on the track to bring a succession of supercars to the roads, each more impressive than the last. The 650S Spider's 3.8 twin-turbo V8 engine bursts into life, accelerating from standing to 60 mph in an eye-watering 3.1 seconds.

DID YOU KNOW?

A special edition of the McLaren 650S called 'One of Seven' has been made. Each car has a special paint effect that makes the car look like a moving bronze sculpture. Snap one up for a cool £290,000!

WOW!

There's no messing about with the retractable hard top. It can be lowered in just 17 seconds, while driving at speeds of up to 30mph.

FAST FACTS

Home Country: United Kingdom

Top Speed: 207 mph (333 kph)

Acceleration: 0–60 in 3.1 seconds

Horsepower: 641

Price: £215,000+

BUGATTI VEYRON SUPER SPORT

5

Wow. That's about all you can say when you see this super-speed monster. Wow. The Bugatti name has been around for more than a century. It was best known for making luxurious classics, but in 2005 they decided to break out, and they did so in style. Most cars today have four cylinders. Some powerful vehicles have eight. Some super-powerful cars even have 12. The Veyron Super Sport has . . . 16! It zips to 60 mph in an eye-wateringly fast 2.5 seconds. No wonder it broke the speed record for the fastest production car in 2010!

WOW!

When the Super Sport hits high speeds, the car goes into handling mode. It lowers so it is very close to the road and a rear wing rises up from the back. The wing improves downforces, which help the car grip the road and corner at high speeds as well as acting like an air brake when the vehicle slows down!

FAST FACTS

Home Country: France

Top Speed: 268 mph (431 kph)

Acceleration: 0–60 in 2.5 seconds

Horsepower: 1,200

Price: £2,100,000

DID YOU KNOW?

In Indonesia, workers created a life-size replica of the Bugatti Veyron SS made entirely from teak wood! It took a month to build and was sold to an exclusive German client for around $3 million.

FERRARI ENZO

6

There are more recent models in the Ferrari stable, but the Enzo is still in pole position for many in their dream supercar list. Designed to celebrate Ferrari's first win on the track after the new millennium, the Enzo brought Formula One technology to the roads, with its six-litre V12 engine.

WOW!

The Enzo can shift gear in an incredible 150 milliseconds – that's about the same amount of time as it takes to blink your eyes!

DID YOU KNOW?

Like an F1 car, the Enzo's gear-change paddles are mounted behind the steering wheel. Lights on the wheel tell the driver when to change gear.

FAST FACTS

Home Country: Italy

Top Speed: 217 mph (349 kph)

Acceleration: 0–60 in 3.6 seconds

Horsepower: 651

Price: £2,006,000 (second-hand!)

PAGANI HUAYRA

7

This Italian supercar replaced Pagani's iconic Zonda, which is a hard act to follow. But the Huayra pulls it off thanks to its stunning, sleek looks and incredible engineering. The car is made from carbotanium – a mix of carbon and titanium – which makes it light, but strong. A six-litre V12 engine shoots from 0–60 in a hair-raising 3.2 seconds. Now that's fast!

FAST FACTS

Home Country: Italy

Top Speed: 230 mph (370 kph)

Acceleration: 0–60 in 3.2 seconds

Horsepower: 730

Price: £800,000

DID YOU KNOW?

The Huayra has two aerodynamic flaps at the front and back, which raise automatically when the car corners, to help with stability.

WOW!

Inside, the car has leather and aluminium detailing. You can choose from the paddle gears behind the wheel or use the gear stick with its exposed mechanism so you can see the 67 moving parts go through the gate as you change gear.

HENNESSEY VENOM GT

8

The design for the Venom GT is based on the Lotus Elise, an iconic sports car from the 1990s. Powered by a twin-turbo seven-litre V8 engine, it has smashed speed records, including fastest acceleration from 0–300 kph (186 mph) in a jaw-dropping 13.63 seconds. Even more impressive when you consider that many saloons take longer than this to accelerate from 0–60 mph!

DID YOU KNOW?

Each car takes six months to make, compared to 18 hours for the average Toyota.

WOW!

The Hennessey Venom F5 is launching in 2016. It's hoped that it may smash the fastest production car records as it's rumoured that it can reach an eye-watering 290 mph.

FAST FACTS

Home Country: United States

Top Speed: 270.5 mph (435 kph)

Acceleration: 0–60 in 2.7 seconds

Horsepower: 1,244

Price: £910,000

FERRARI LAFERRARI

9

LaFerrari is the successor to the Enzo and possibly one of the slickest hybrid hypercars to hit the roads. Packing a massive 6.3-litre V12 engine, along with a rear axle powered by an electric motor, this car has serious thrust, accelerating from 0–60 in less than three seconds. Yet with a run of just 499 vehicles, the chance of seeing one of these beauties on the road is rare.

DID YOU KNOW?

The driving position in a LaFerrari is pretty similar to that of an F1 car – seats are low-slung so your backside is almost on the floor!

WOW!

The electric motor adds the equivalent of an ordinary saloon's horsepower to the engine. But unlike some hybrids, LaFerrari cannot be driven in purely electric mode, and on the plus side, it doesn't need charging!

FAST FACTS

Home Country: Italy

Top Speed: 227 mph (365 kph)

Acceleration: 0–60 in 2.9 seconds

Horsepower: 950

Price: £1,000,000

SHELBY SUPER CAR (SSC) ULTIMATE AERO TT

10

Before the Bugatti Veyron roared onto the scene, the Ultimate Aero was the fastest production car in the world, thanks to its 6.3-litre twin-turbo V8 engine that shoots from 0–60 in an awe-inspiring 2.8 seconds! The Ultimate Aero boasts ultra-modern scissor doors and extra-wide tyres to help it hold the road at high speed.

WOW!

The Ultimate Aero has brake-deployed rear spoilers, for better stopping power.

FAST FACTS

Home Country: United States

Top Speed: 257 mph (414 kph)

Acceleration: 0–60 in 2.8 seconds

Horsepower: 1,287

Price: £500,000

DID YOU KNOW?

There's no rear-view mirror in the Ultimate Aero. Luckily, drivers are provided with a rear camera instead, as well as a 10-speaker sound system!

HIDDEN CARS

Can you track down the following cool cars in this wordsearch?

v	t	u	r	b	a	r	n	v	e	r	n	j	x	w	o
u	e	h	a	r	m	i	r	a	r	r	e	f	a	l	r
l	z	y	r	n	p	u	a	k	s	r	x	u	r	a	r
k	x	a	r	s	r	x	o	b	r	u	t	o	y	f	p
a	o	r	p	o	j	e	x	v	s	a	i	n	a	l	m
e	r	y	y	o	n	e	b	a	a	t	p	l	u	v	o
v	e	a	m	r	t	s	a	s	g	f	y	y	h	p	n
o	a	u	a	y	a	p	u	a	z	e	e	d	z	x	e
p	e	f	v	k	m	e	o	p	p	l	r	o	d	p	v
o	t	e	e	i	o	e	p	z	e	a	i	a	x	s	r
r	a	r	n	o	e	d	o	x	n	r	e	e	h	p	r
s	m	a	t	r	x	b	r	o	z	t	s	i	b	i	o
c	i	r	a	r	a	y	s	r	o	a	r	p	s	d	j
h	t	o	d	p	a	o	h	z	u	d	y	u	o	e	m
e	l	r	o	s	a	i	n	w	l	o	k	p	s	r	a
z	u	v	r	o	p	e	d	s	a	i	u	y	i	z	t

Agera	LaFerrari	Turbo
Aventador	Porsche	Ultimate Aero
Enzo	Speed	Venom
Huayra	Spider	Veyron Super Sport

CHAPTER 4
THE NEED FOR SPEED!

As soon as different makes and models of car were made, people started to pit them against each other, racing to see which was the fastest and the best. Just as there are many types of car, there are all sorts of ways of racing, too. Here's a look at some of the most famous, amazing, and yes, super-fast racing circuits from all over the world!

FORMULA ONE (F1)

The FIA Formula One World Championship is a season of races held in different countries. Each race is called a Grand Prix. Some races are held on tracks, while others are on the streets of major cities. Drivers from 14 countries have won the annual championship.

The Rules

Formula One's name means that all the cars must be built from the same formula, or plan. They are 'open-wheel' cars, which means their tyres are not covered by parts of the car. F1 cars also have open cockpits with a single seat, for the driver. Drivers earn points in every F1 race, with the winners getting the most points, of course. The season champion is the driver with most points from all the races.

Star Drivers

Michael Schumacher
This German star won an amazing seven F1 championships, including five in a row (2000–2004). His best season was 2004, when he won 13 out of 18 races.

Juan Manuel Fangio
From Argentina, Fangio was the sport's first hero. He won five of the first eight championships.

Sebastian Vettel
This young German is one of the hottest F1 drivers today. He won four championships in a row from 2010 to 2013.

Magic Moments

- The 1971 Italian Grand Prix ended with five cars finishing within a second of each other!

- When an F1 car decelerates, the force is so great it would be like driving a regular car through a brick wall – at 186 mph (300 kph)!

FAST FACTS

First Season: 1950
Number of Races: 20 (2015)
Type of Tracks: Street-like circuits
Most Championships: Michael Schumacher – seven

- Pit stop crews take just 3 seconds to refuel and change a set of tyres.

Most Famous Race

Monaco Grand Prix: Every F1 driver dreams of winning this race, as the Monte Carlo circuit is the hardest of the F1 tracks, thanks to the city's narrow streets, hairpin bends and tunnel. Many wealthy fans moor their yachts in the harbour to watch the cars shoot past.

NASCAR

NASCAR stands for National Association for Stock Car Auto Racing. A 'stock' car means a standard production line car that you might be able to buy and drive. Today, NASCAR cars are built just for racing, though their body styles are still based on everyday passenger cars.

The Rules

During NASCAR's 36-race season, drivers are tested on short tracks of half a mile or less, mile-long ovals, and superspeedways that are more than two miles around. They also race twice on curvy, twisting road courses. Drivers build up points in each race depending on where they finish and by how many laps they lead. Any driver who wins a race earns a spot in the season-ending 10-race 'Chase for the Cup'. As those 10 races are run, drivers are eliminated until four survive for a final-race dash for the championship.

FAST FACTS

First Season: 1948
Number of Races: 36
Type of Tracks: short tracks, ovals, superspeedways and road courses
Most Championships: Richard Petty and Dale Earnhardt Sr – seven each

Star Drivers

Richard Petty

'The King' won a record 200 races and seven NASCAR championships.

Dale Earnhardt Sr

Called 'The Man in Black' for his car colour and fierce attitude, he won seven NASCAR titles, too. Sadly, he was killed in a crash in the 2001 Daytona 500.

Jeff Gordon

He was one of the youngest NASCAR champs, and then won three more titles. His 92 race wins are among the most ever.

Magic Moments

• The first NASCAR race was held in Florida in 1948, on a course that was partly on the sand of Daytona Beach!

• The Disney film *Cars* was inspired by NASCAR – the character of 'The King' is voiced by NASCAR's own 'King' Richard Petty!

• The first woman to earn a starting spot was Janet Guthrie, who in 1977 raced in the Indianapolis 500 and Daytona 500, where she was Top Rookie!

Most Famous Race

The Daytona 500 started in 1959 at Florida's Daytona International Speedway. It has become NASCAR's biggest race, kicking off each season on its huge 2.5-mile track. Not surprisingly, Richard Petty has won the most times, with seven victories from 1964 to 1981.

INDYCAR

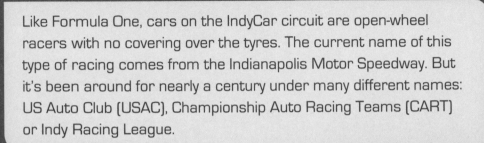

Like Formula One, cars on the IndyCar circuit are open-wheel racers with no covering over the tyres. The current name of this type of racing comes from the Indianapolis Motor Speedway. But it's been around for nearly a century under many different names: US Auto Club (USAC), Championship Auto Racing Teams (CART) or Indy Racing League.

The Rules

Like Formula One, the drivers sit in open cockpits. Large wings on the back of the cars help drivers control the high-speed cars. Drivers pile up points in an annual series of 19 races held on ovals, permanent road courses and temporary street courses. Most races are held in the United States, with one race each in Canada and Brazil during the 2015 season.

Most Famous Race

The Indy 500 might just be the most famous car race in the world. It's certainly one of the oldest, with the first held in 1911. The Indianapolis Motor Speedway is known as the Brickyard, as that was what the early roadway was made from.

Star Drivers

A. J. Foyt

Foyt was one of America's most successful drivers. He was the first to win four Indy 500s, and is the only driver to hold more than 20 wins in all four USAC divisions: IndyCar; stock cars; sprint cars and midget cars.

Mario Andretti

A champion racer across the board, Andretti is one of only two drivers to have won NASCAR, IndyCar, World Sportscar Championship AND F1! His IndyCar wins stretch across four decades. In 2000 he and A. J. Foyt were jointly named 'Driver of the Century'.

FAST FACTS

First Season: 1911
Number of Races: 16 (2015)
Type of Tracks: ovals, permanent and temporary road courses
Most Championships: A. J. Foyt, Mario Andretti, Sebastien Bourdais, Dario Franchitti – four each

Magic Moments

• In 1936, Louis Mayer had a post-race drink of buttermilk in the victory lane. It started a tradition that's still followed by Indy 500 winners today.

• The fastest Indy 500 was completed in 1990 by Dutch driver Arie Lyendyk, with a time of 2 hours 41 minutes 18.4 seconds!

• At the 1992 Indy 500, Al Unser Jr. beat Michael Andretti in the closest finish ever: there was only 0.043 seconds between them!

DRAG RACING

Drag racing is the fastest motor sport. At its top races, drivers reach more than 300 mph (483 kph) in specially made cars. They don't race for long, though. Most races only last a few seconds! Drag racing's roots are on the streets, where car fans used to duel to see who had the fastest car in town. Today, the National Hot Rod Association (NHRA) makes the rules and crowns the champs.

The Rules

NHRA drag races happen on a short track that's usually around 200 to 400 metres ($\frac{1}{8}$ to $\frac{1}{4}$ of a mile) long. Each race has only two cars, with winners advancing round by round to a championship. The famous 'Christmas tree' of lights signals drivers to start. Parachutes are needed to help the mighty machines slow down at the end of each race.

FAST FACTS

First Season: 1953
Number of Races: 24
Type of Tracks: Drag strips
Most Championships:
Tony Schumacher, 8 (Top Fuel);
John Force, 16 (Funny Car);
Bob Glidden, 10 (Pro Stock)

accident, he pioneered the 'top-fuel dragster', which was safer for drivers, as the engine was placed at the back.

Star Drivers

"Big Daddy" Don Garlits won 17 championships in all sorts of different drag racers, smashing many speed records. After an

Shirley "Cha Cha" Muldowney became the first woman ever to be a national driving champion when she won the Top Fuel title in 1977.

Main Types of Drag Races

There are hundreds of different classes of drag racing, all over the world, but the main three are:

Top Fuel

Powered by nitromethane, not petrol, Top Fuel cars are designed just for drag racing. They are 7.6 metres (25 feet) long and sport massive rear wheels and tiny front wheels. The driver sits behind the massive engine. At the start, the tyres spin and smoke before catching and sending the car zooming down the straightway. Top Fuel dragsters are the fastest in the world, accelerating from 0 to 100 mph in a jaw-dropping 0.8 seconds – that's three times as fast as most supercars! From a standing start, dragsters can accelerate faster than a Formula One car or a fighter jet, and set off with the same amount of force as the rocket used to launch the US Space Shuttle!

Pro Stock

Also called 'factory hot-rods', these cars are designed much more like 'regular' cars. They have four tyres of similar size, but they also have massive engines. They 'only' go at 220 mph (354 kph).

Funny Cars

Also known as 'floppers' funny cars are shorter versions of Top Fuel cars. They also have a complete fibreglass body cover, while Top Fuel cars have an open cockpit. Like Top Fuel, these cars can top 315 mph (506 kph).

OFF-ROAD AND RALLY DRIVING

Racing is not just for tracks and speedways. Daring drivers also battle each other on dirt roads, rough tracks, desert sands and just about anywhere you can squeeze a car. One of the most famous types of 'off-road' racing is rally driving. This is especially popular in Europe.

The Rules

The big difference between rally racing and other types is the tracks. The cars are still fast, and they are often souped-up versions of regular street cars. But the tracks don't go round and round... they go one way. In the World Rally Championship (WRC for short), the driving is divided up into 15 to 25 stages. These are short courses on closed roads on terrain as variable as desert scrub, snow or alpine forests. Teams must complete them in the fastest possible time. Between each stage, they drive on regular roads and must stick to the road rules. To add to the drama, once a rally has started, the driver and navigator are not allowed help from their team. If they break down, they must fix the car themselves!

FAST FACTS

First Season: 1973
Number of Races: 13
Type of Tracks: Dirt, gravel, roads, snow, desert and even ice!
Most Championships: Sebastian Loeb – nine

Star Drivers

Juha Kankkunen

Kankkunen from Finland won four World Rally Championships titles. In 2011, he also set a speed record for driving on ice in a Bentley Continental Supersports convertible, racking up a super-slidey speed of 205 mph (330 kph)!

Sebastian Loeb

Loeb dominated WRC in the 2000s. The Frenchman won his first drivers' title in 2004 ... and then won eight more in a row!

Most Famous Race

The Paris-Dakar Rally (or 'The Dakar' for short) is not part of the WRC, but it's the most famous off-road race in the world. Originally, the rally started in Paris, France, and competitors drove all the way to Dakar, in Senegal, covering more than 6,200 miles (10,000 km) across every terrain you can imagine. Cars, motorcycles, trucks and desert buggies all take part. From 2009, the race moved to South America, due to problems in Mauritania. Now, the race runs in a loop from Buenos Aires in Argentina, into Chile and Bolivia and back to Buenos Aires.

V8 SUPERCARS CHAMPIONSHIP (AUSTRALIA)

Australia's favourite motor sport is this action-packed series. Imagine high-speed cars, like in NASCAR, racing in tight curves, like Formula One. That's a recipe for bumper-banging, lightning-fast action that delights fans all around the world. The series has been around since 1960, but only known as the V8 Supercars Championship since 2003.

The Rules

Drivers compete in all the races in a season, piling up points based on their finishes. Races are held on road and street circuits, but some, called 'endurance races', are so long that teams of two drivers take turns. The cars look sort of like 'street' cars, but use powerful V8 engines (hence the name!).

Most Famous Race

The Bathurst 1000 (also known as The Great Race) takes nearly seven hours to complete. Two-man teams of drivers swap during the 160-plus laps of the huge 1,000 km course. It's been run since 1960.

Star Drivers

Jamie Whincup

Whincup has won a record six V8 championships, including winning every year from 2011 to 2014.

Craig Lowndes

Lowndes has won 97 V8 races, more than any other driver, and three season titles.

DRIFTING

In drifting, cars don't race just for speed, they race for style! As drivers go round the track, they deliberately oversteer when they corner so that the car loses traction. The rear of the car slides to the side, but in spite of the smoke and drama, the driver is still in control and, rather than spin right round, the car still corners! Drivers follow a line on the circuit and are awarded points for this, as well as the angle of the drift, the amount of smoke and the crowd's reaction.

The Rules

The cars are basically the same ones you see on the street, usually with some modifications like a roll cage for safety.

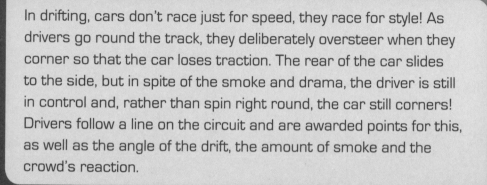

Star Drivers

Keiichi Tsuchiya

Also known as the 'Drift King', Tsuchiya has helped make the sport popular through his work in movies and TV.

Chris Forsberg

In the USA, drifting has its own series, called 'Formula Drift' or Formula D. Chris Forsberg has been a part of every Formula D season and has won two championships.

FAST FACTS

First Season: 2000 (Japan)
Number of Rounds: 7
Type of Tracks: Special drifting-only layouts
Most Championships: Youichi Imamura – two D1 titles

History Lesson

Drifting began in mountain racing in Japan in the 1970s and 1980s. Now it's one of the biggest sports in the country, with it's own D1 Grand Prix. The sport's popularity spread throughout the world, thanks in part to movies and TV shows.

FASTEST STREET-LEGAL CARS

The cars you've read about in this chapter are all created to race on special tracks under specific series rules. They can't do their stuff on city streets. However, some other super-fast cars are allowed on normal roads around the world. They can drive mega-fast on motorways... but they'll probably be breaking the law! We have already met three of the fastest street-legal cars – the Hennessey Venom GT, the Bugatti Veyron Super Sport and the Pagani Huayra. Now let's check out some of the competition:

KOENIGSEGG ONE:1

Koenigsegg's One:1 was unveiled at the 2014 Geneva Motor Show. Achieving a top speed of 273 mph (439 kph) with its twin-turbo 5.0-litre V8 engine, this car can do some serious stuff. But don't get your wallet out just yet – the run is limited to six and all of them have been snapped up!

ZENVO ST1

Denmark cracks the top ranks of speed with the Zenvo ST1. They don't make many of them, so they can pour in the speed. Its V8 engine can hit 233 mph (375 kph)!

FAST FACT

How are these cars tested? Experts and scientists get to take thrilling rides while they examine machines that measure the cars' speed. Car magazines and TV shows also like to create challenges to find new speed kings as they put these monster machines through their paces.

SALEEN S7 TWIN-TURBO

Its smooth, sleek looks hide a massive V8 engine that can shoot from 0 to 60 in an awe-inspiring 2.8 seconds, topping out at an incredible 248 mph (399 kph). This isn't a car for the faint-hearted!

A TEST OF SPEED!

You've just read about some really fast cars. Now let's test your speed. You'll need some paper, a pen and maybe a stopwatch (or a timer on your phone) to take on these challenges.

1. In 30 seconds, how many different car companies can you name... without repeating any?

2. Next time you're travelling, have a competition with your friends and family. Give each person (except the driver, he or she needs to concentrate!) a make of car such as Ford or Volkswagen. See how many each of you can spot during the journey. The winner is the person with the highest score.

3. Grab a small toy car for each of your friends and take them somewhere to race – a path in the park is ideal, especially if it slopes downhill! See who can make the longest run, and whose car is fastest. Take a selection of different cars and set up your own drag races, with the winning car going through to the next round!

4. Why not invent your own supersonic sports car? On a piece of paper, draw your ultimate dream machine. Does it include extras like turbo jets, go-faster stripes or is it fuelled by the Sun's rays? Let your imagination go wild!

CHAPTER 5
WORLD OF WHEELS

There are more than a billion cars driving on Earth's roads. Thankfully they're not all in one place, or it would be a very long, boring traffic jam! Luckily they're spread pretty much throughout the world's roads, but most of them are produced by just a few countries. The major car-producing countries each have their top sellers, and some become popular outside their home country, too. Here's a road trip through the international world of wheels!

Cars were not invented in the US... but they quickly became popular, as the car was the perfect way to explore America's wide-open spaces. Over the past century, cars of every size and style have roared along American roads.

American Car Facts

• If you're itching to get your licence, America is the place to be. In most states you can learn to drive when you are 16.

• In America, as well as getting drive-through fast food, you can go to the drive-through bank or even have a drive-through wedding! In the 1950s and 1960s, you could go to a drive-in movie theatre and watch the latest Hollywood blockbuster without leaving your driver's seat!

• The US President's limousine is nicknamed 'The Beast'. Designed to protect the President from attack, it has bullet-proof windows, armour-plating and tyres that will run and run, even if they are punctured.

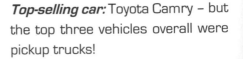

Top-selling car: Toyota Camry – but the top three vehicles overall were pickup trucks!

Famous Brands

- Buick
- Cadillac
- Chevrolet
- Chrysler
- Dodge
- Ford
- General Motors
- Lincoln
- Mercury
- Plymouth
- Oldsmobile
- Tesla

The Ultimate American Car!

We had thousands to choose from, but this wasn't really a hard choice. Nothing looks more like an American car than the 1957 Chevy Bel Air. Big and beautiful, it's an all-time classic.

GREAT BRITAIN

Britain did not jump into car culture as fast as the United States. But British car-makers became known for making quality cars with luxury brands such as Rolls-Royce and Jaguar. Meanwhile, the regular car market was dominated by iconic brands such as MG sports cars, Austin and Rover, as well as Mini Cooper, the car that everyone associates with London and the 1960s!

British Car Facts

• 'British Racing Green' is the classic colour of choice for British sports cars, both on the road and the race track!

• In Britain, once you hit 17 you can get your own wheels, but first you must pass TWO driving tests. A theory test to make sure you know the rules of the road – AKA the 'Highway Code' – and a practical driving test.

• Up until 1975, even though indicators were pretty standard in cars, people still had to show they knew how to do hand signals as part of the driving test.

• The most popular car colour in Britain? White!

• One of the best sports cars of the last 30 years is British: the Lotus Elise.

Top-selling car: Ford Fiesta.

Famous Brands

- Aston Martin
- Bentley
- Jaguar
- Land Rover
- McLaren
- Rolls-Royce
- Lotus

The Ultimate British Car!

So many great cars to choose from! Is it James Bond's Aston Martin? The Queen's Bentley? We looked at them all, but chose the Jaguar E-type. It was made from 1961 to 1975 as a two-seater, usually a convertible. It has a long, low front that is unlike any other sports car. Order one for us in British racing green!

Cars have been made in France since the 1890s. Only a few companies still make cars there, but the brands Renault, Citroën and Peugeot are known around the world.

French Car Facts

• France was the top car-maker in Europe until 1933, when Great Britain overtook it.

• Probably one of the quirkiest cars to come out of France was Citroën's 2CV. This tiny but tough car was first designed after World War II and became a firm favourite both in France and abroad. Early models had tiny 9 horsepower engines and could drive 100 km on 3 litres of fuel!

• In France, you have to wait until you are 18 years old to drive on their roads. So even if you pass your driving test in the UK at 17, you'll still have to wait another year before you book that trip across the Channel!

Top-selling car: Renault Clio IV.

Famous Brands

- Bugatti
- Citroën
- Peugeot
- Renault

The Ultimate French Car!

The Citroën has a shape unlike any other car. A long, flat curve from front to back marks this car instantly as part of French culture. The DS has self-levelling suspension. When the car starts, the back rises up to a pre-selected height. Cool! The company made different models for decades, but the DS is perhaps the most famous. It came in third place in the 2000 Car of the Century award.

ITALY

When car fans think of Italy, they think of sports cars. Led by Ferrari, Italian sports cars have long been among the fastest and most famous in the world. Drivers love putting these these small, sports cars through their paces, especially on Italy's many twisting mountain roads and thrilling hairpin bends.

Italian Car Facts

• Fiat is by far the biggest brand in Italy. In some years, its cars make up 90 percent of Italian cars made. It's no surprise, therefore that Fiat have won European Car of the Year more times than any other car-maker!

• Enzo Ferrari created his first cars in 1929 and his name has been on fabulous sports cars ever since. But his company is now part of Fiat, too.

• The Fiat 500 was Italy's post-war small, economical car. It was nicknamed 'Topolino' which means 'little mouse'. The 500 has recently made a comeback, but this version has a few more luxuries, including an optional coffee machine!

Top-selling car: Fiat Panda.

Famous Brands

- Alfa Romeo
- Ferrari
- Fiat
- Lamborghini
- Maserati
- Pagani

The Ultimate Italian Car!

Ferrari is the most famous Italian car name – no argument. But which Ferrari is the classic? We're going with the iconic 250 GTO, with its 12-cylinder 3-litre engine, which produced 300 horsepower and a top speed of 170 mph. It might seem tame compared to today's supercars, but many enthusiasts still believe this is the finest in the Ferrari stable. Only 39 of these beauties were made and Enzo Ferrari approved each sale himself! Today, one would set you back around £34 million ($50 million). Gulp!

GERMANY

Germany can be said to be the birthplace of cars, thanks to Karl Benz (see page 8 for more info). In the decades since his invention, Germans have become great car engineers. German cars are known for their solid build and excellent quality. No surprise then that alongside the US, China and Japan it is one of the world's top car manufacturers, in part due to its luxury brands such as Mercedes and Porsche.

German Car Facts

• Germany is home to the Nürburgring, one of the most famous racing road courses in the world.

• Many petrolheads love German roads and in particular the motorways or 'autobahns'. Why? Because it's one of the few places in the world where you can really see what speed a car can do without getting a ticket – some sections have no speed limit at all!

• If you want to test out those autobahns for yourself, you'll have a longer wait. In Germany you have to be 18 to drive.

Top-selling car: Volkswagen Golf

Famous Brands

- Audi
- BMW
- Gumpert
- Mercedes-Benz
- Opel
- Porsche
- Volkswagen

The Ultimate German Car!

Some say this is the best Mercedes ever made. It's certainly one of the most sought-after German sports cars! Classic lines and futuristic gullwing doors made the Mercedes 300SL a car that most people could only dream of owning in the 1950s. By today's standards its top speed of 135 mph looks quite sedate, but even so, this stylish sports coupé can fetch anything up to £2.5 million ($3.7 million) for one of the rarer models.

SWEDEN

Swedish cars are designed to cope with very cold driving conditions, including ice and snow. And their cars also have a great reputation for safety. In particular, Volvo cars are chosen by many because of their solid build and high-spec safety features.

Sweden Car Facts

• Sweden used to drive on the left side of the road, as in Britain. But in 1967, they switched, which made for a chaotic few days on the roads!

• In Sweden, it's the law that you must drive with your headlights on, even on a bright sunny day. It's not surprising then to find out that most cars sold there have no on-off switch for lights, they come on automatically when you start the engine!

Top-selling car: Volvo V70

Famous Brands

- Saab
- Volvo
- Koenigsegg

The Ultimate Swedish Car!

The Volvo V70 is one of the most well known of Swedish cars and is still a bestseller. Loved by families for its TARDIS-like interior as well as its safety features, it's the perfect car for whizzing through town or eating up the miles on holiday. Some might say that its boxy design is a little dull, but it sells and sells!

JAPAN

Japan has made cars for more than a century. In the 1970s, when worldwide oil prices shot up, people needed smaller cars that used less petrol. Japan was ahead of the game with their compact cars that were ideal for city driving. Today, Japan is the third-biggest car-making country in the world. It's also the home of many top motorcycle brands.

Japanese Car Facts

• Cars in Japan are pretty cheap to buy, but running them is expensive. There's fuel, insurance, but hardest of all is parking. In Tokyo, you have to have a parking space before you get a car. Space is at such a premium that there are more than 1.6 million car parking spaces in Japan where electronic stacking is used as it's the most efficient way to squeeze in as many cars as possible!

• In Japan, you have to be 18 before you can get behind a wheel. At least it gives you time to save for a parking space!

• Six of the top 10 bestselling cars in America are Japanese.

Top-selling car: Toyota Aqua

Famous Brands

- Daihatsu
- Honda
- Isuzu
- Mazda
- Mitsubishi
- Nissan
- Subaru
- Suzuki
- Toyota

The Ultimate Japanese Car!

Talk about a success story! Since its launch in 1966, the Toyota Corolla has become the biggest-selling car of all time. More than 40 million have been sold since then.

KOREA

South Korea had a late start in the world car market. It was not until the 1950s that factories there started making their own cars. By the 1980s, Hyundai and, later, Kia led the way in taking Korean cars to other countries, too.

Korean Car Facts

• Though a small country, Korea is the fifth-largest car-maker in the world.

Top-selling car: Hyundai Sonata

• In South Korea, taxis are colour-coded. If you hail a grey or white cab, you will get a basic car with a driver who is qualified but not experienced. Hail a black car if you want luxury with a more experienced driver – at a higher price, of course!

• In South Korea you can get a driver's licence when you turn 18.

Famous Brands

- Hyundai

- Kia

The Ultimate Korean Car!

While other countries have ultimate cars with flash, speed, style or history, South Korea's is pretty plain. But the Hyundai Sonata (also known as the Hyundai i45) represents its homeland well. It's very popular around the world, well made and affordable. For a country still waiting for a great sports car, this is a solid winner

OPEN UP YOUR WALLET

Cars are one of the most expensive purchases most people will make. But some people can afford to pay more than others. They buy the highest-priced cars on the market. Why? It's almost like buying into a very exclusive club. Some, as we have seen in the supercars pages, are so exclusive that the car companies decide who gets to buy! What you get for your money is a hand-made vehicle that positively reeks of luxury, with all sorts of fancy additions such as the softest leather seats, and precision-made parts. Let's take a look at some of these big-ticket buys.

Porsche 918 Spyder

You want to save the Earth *and* have a super-expensive car? We've got your wheels here. This Porsche has a hybrid engine, combining a V8 engine with an electric powertrain. You can feel good about yourself while hitting 60 mph (97 kph) in 2.5 seconds. Of course, to feel that good, you have to spend around £600,000 ($900,000), depending on which extras you pick!

Lamborghini Venono Roadster

If you have an extra £3.3 million ($4.9 million) lying around, you could consider shelling out for this ultra-luxurious supercar. It's got a mighty 6.5-litre, V12 engine, that shoots from 0–60 in 2.9 seconds. Coupled with its awesome styling and carbon-fibre body for lightweight strength, this supercar is something else. Snap one of these up and you'll be in a super-exclusive club, as only nine are being made!

Bugatti Veyron 16.4 Grand Sport Vitesse

This super-cool contender is the tweaked version of the Super Sport we met in The Cool Car Collection on page 40. With beefed-up twin-turbos and intercoolers, the Grand Sport Vitesse has a top speed of 258 mph and produces a massive 1,200 horsepower. Unsurprisingly, the word 'Vitesse' means 'speed'. But if you want to snap up one of these beauties, you'll have to shell out a cool £1.7 million ($2.5 million).

FAST FACTS

When cars are put on display to sell, usually the dealer puts a large sign in the window. The sign lists all the features of the car, along with the price to buy it. But if you're buying a big-ticket item, the most you may see is a discreet sign saying 'POA' – 'price on application' – which can be a polite way of saying if you need to ask the price, you probably can't afford it!

THE WEIRD AND WONDERFUL

Let's look at some of the quirkiest cars that have ever hit the roads. From cars made of plastic (yes, really!) to ones without a reverse gear, take a look at some of the weirdest and most wonderful vehicles.

The Stout Scarab

In 1936, aircraft designer William Stout launched the Scarab, a car powered by a Ford truck engine that was meant to bring some luxury to the roads. In many ways it was ahead of its time, as it had lots of innovative features as well as the space and flexibility of a camper van, with seats that could be moved around and even a pull-down table! Sadly, it didn't take off, partly because it was so expensive to buy – a new one cost the equivalent of around £61,600 ($90,000) in today's money.

The Amphicar

Is it a boat? Is it a car? Well, it's both actually. The Amphicar (amphibious car) was based on the Triumph Herald, with twin propellers mounted under the back bumper to power it in water. Powered by a four-cylinder 43 bhp (brake horsepower) engine, the car could achieve a respectable 70 mph (113 kph) on land. Unfortunately, it was expensive, and as it was sold in the US market, its tiny engine just couldn't compete with the muscle cars of the 1960s.

The Peel P50

In the 1950s and 60s, as well as the iconic Mini, there were many other tiny cars on the road, including futuristic bubble cars. One of the smallest to be made was the Peel P50, which launched in 1963. This one-cylinder engine had a top speed of 38 mph (61 kph), and just enough room for a driver and a small shopping bag. The gear box had three speeds and no reverse, but luckily the manufacturers had thought about that and the car came with a nifty handle on the back so instead of doing a three-point turn, all the driver had to do was pick it up and turn it round!

THE PEEL P50   THE TRABANT   THE AMPHICAR

The Trabant

First on anyone's list of unusual cars has to be the Trabant, or 'Trabi' as it is affectionately known. Because yes, believe it or not, it has its fans! But these car enthusiasts are not looking for speed or looks, which is just as well, as the humble Trabi has a two-stroke engine and just 26 horsepower, and was known for being noisy and belching out thick black smoke. With a body made of Duroplast, a type of reinforced plastic, it was very, very lightweight. The Trabi was born in communist East Germany and was, for a long time, the only car available. In spite of its drawbacks, the waiting list was years long.

CARS OF THE FUTURE

So what will car-makers do next in their quest to bring new technology and cutting-edge design to the roads? Let's take a look at some of the innovations that are being worked on as we speak.

Where's the Driver?

Robots are used in factories, offices and hospitals. Many car-makers are dreaming up ways to use the technology on our roads in the form of driverless cars. Someday soon, a motorway trip may involve nothing more than putting your feet up and reading, while the car does the work for you!

Go, Go, Google!

Google, the search-engine company, is currently experimenting with driverless cars, with prototypes which are modified ordinary cars being road-tested in the US and Europe. Google's millions of miles of online maps help the cars know where to go. Sensors 'read' the road and the world around the car. Google has also showcased a driverless pod, where there are two seats and nothing else apart from two buttons, one to start it and an emergency stop. Watch this space!

Blind Drivers?

In 2009, students at Virginia Tech University in the US made a car that can be driven by a blind person. Unlike driverless cars, the driver is still in control. The technology 'reads' the road, giving the driver feedback so they can manuoevre the car.

No Bus Driver?

The city of Lyon, France, is experimenting with a driverless minibus. They operate (slowly!) in the city streets, taking passengers on a pre-planned route, using lasers rather than sensors to help them find their way around.

Pros & Cons

Some people think the driverless car is a great idea. Other people are not so sure. Here are some of the pros and cons.

Pros

• Computers are smarter than people. They can react more quickly, too.

• Trucks/lorries with robot drivers will be able to let human drivers rest on long trips.

• Some experts say the cars will be safer and reduce accidents.

Cons

• No computer can be ready for every possible emergency.

• Trucks with robot drivers might not need humans so people might lose their jobs.

• What if someone hacked the car's system and took it over?

ZOOM INTO THE FUTURE

In the last 130 years or so cars have changed so much that they are virtually unrecognizable. So where do they go next? Will they fly? Go underwater? Travel underground? Who knows...

Alternative Fuel

Some car companies are developing hydrogen cars and Toyota is leading the way with the launch of its first hydrogen cell car, the Mirai. The best thing about hydrogen car is that the only thing they give off is steam. Now that's good news for the planet!

TOYOTA MIRAI

MERCEDES BIOME

Growing a Car?

Mercedes-Benz has come up with a concept to grow cars! The Mercedes Biome would be completely recyclable and would be grown from seeds. The only emission it would give off would be oxygen. Sounds amazing!